Life according to
GUINEA PIGS

A STUDIO PRESS BOOK

First published in the UK in 2020 by Studio Press,
an imprint of Bonnier Books UK,
The Plaza, 535 King's Road, London SW10 0SZ
Owned by Bonnier Books, Sveavägen 56, Stockholm, Sweden

www.studiopressbooks.co.uk
www.bonnierbooks.co.uk

© Studio Press Books, 2020
Photography © Lysanne Robben, *Guinea Pigs Adventures*™, 2020

1 3 5 7 9 10 8 6 4 2
All rights reserved
ISBN 978-1-78741-749-6

Written by Ellie Ross
Edited by Sophie Blackman
Designed by Nia Williams

@guineapigsadventures

A CIP catalogue for this book is available from the British Library.
Printed and bound in China.

Life according to
GUINEA PIGS

Written by
Ellie Ross

STUDIO
PRESS

When you make a jus
instead of gravy.

When your mum answers
a FaceTime call.

When you're off to meet
the in-laws.

When Lady and the Tramp is goals but you don't eat carbs.

When you pronounce it 'choritho'.

When one person at yoga is way more advanced.

When you're getting in from a night out and the sun is coming up.

When you do an ancestry
test and discover your
great-grandfather
was half Irish.

When you ignore your friends' advice to play it cool.

When you've been
on the inflatable for
nearly ten minutes
and no one's taken
a photo yet.

When your 5K run turns into
a 1K stroll to the shops for a
bag of Skips and a full-fat Coke.

When you've given up
dairy and the table
next to you orders
cheesecake.

When your iPhone
finally learns that
you are never typing
'ducking'.

When the date was awful but you'd do anything to avoid an awkward goodbye.

When you're going
out out.

When someone you have no intention of seeing again asks you your name.

When your vegan friend is served anything with nut milk.

When you're in the club toilets and you hear your friend in the cubicle next door.

When writing a to-do list is the only thing you've accomplished on your to-do list.

When you drink and face mask.

When you remove yourself
from the drama.

When you've spent
five minutes being
outdoorsy and are
wondering when
you can stop.

When she says everything's fine.

When your date says they're attracted to people who don't play by the rules.

When you don't read the wedding
invite until you're outside the
church and have to get creative
with 'hats encouraged!'

When your iPhone tells you how many hours of screen time you've had this week.

When you're meant to be doing positive affirmations in the mirror but you've spent half an hour wondering if your face is symmetrical.

When the CBD
kicks in.

When the person who told you they weren't looking for anything serious updates their Facebook status to 'engaged'.

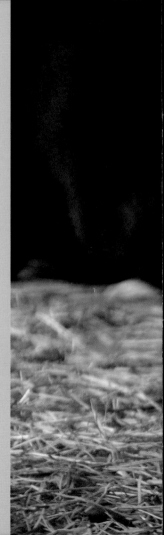

When you try to get a group pic...

... after a bottomless brunch.

When you're wondering if 94 hen do posts is too many hen do posts.

When you forgot about
the weird thing you
ordered at 2a.m.
last Friday.

When you read one Instagram post on climate change.

When you're aware you only pray when you're asking for something but you really need God to make them text you back.

When you read
the Culture section
of the paper.

When you're five beers down and Segways seem like a good idea.

When your therapist suggests you immerse yourself in nature.

When you're having a bath
and you hear a noise downstairs.

When someone suggests
a spin class.

When someone asks
what you want
from life.

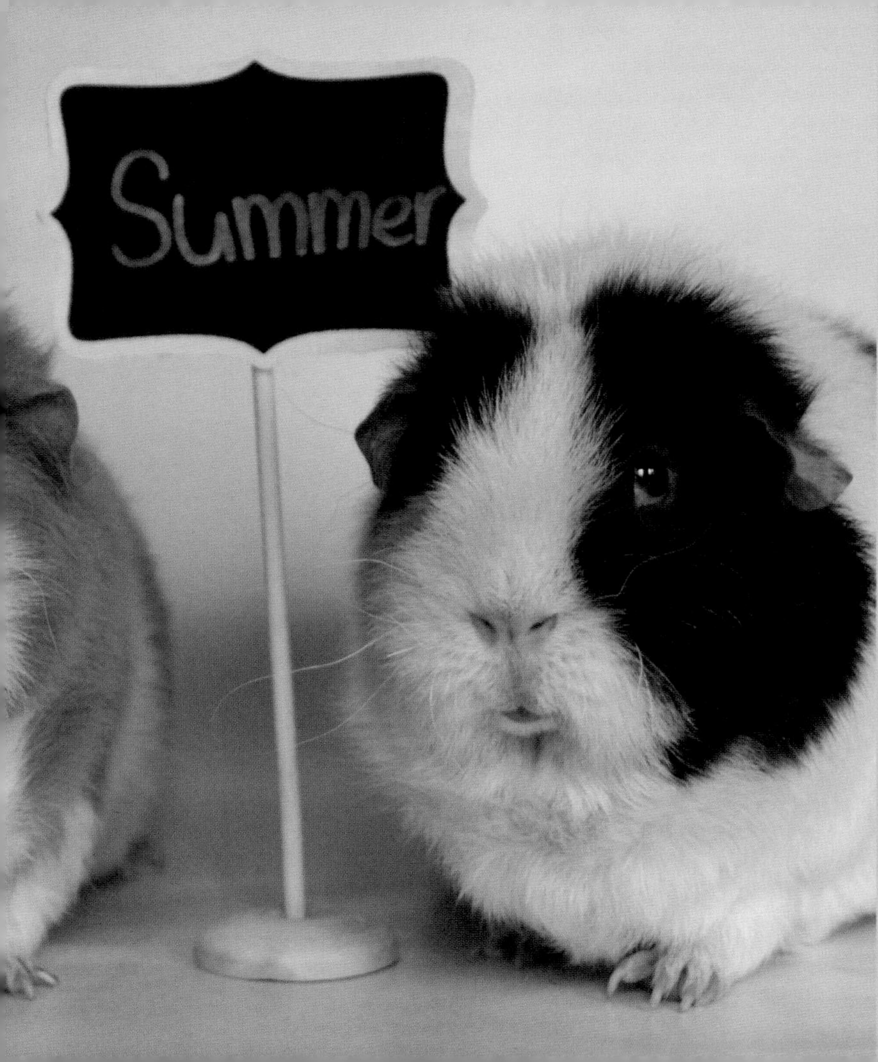
Summer

When someone gets on
the table at a party
but it's way too early.

When you decide Halloween is a capitalist holiday invented for commercial gain that celebrates evil and promotes unhealthy sugar consumption, then October 31st arrives.

When your mum says she doesn't have a favourite but you all know the truth.

When you take up a hobby to relax and have never been more stressed.

When the waitress takes your plate with a halloumi fry left on it.

When her Tinder bio says 'looking for Prince Charming'.

When it's 3a.m. and 'Wonderwall' comes on.

When you convince your friend to break Dry January.

When you check to see how many of your 10,000 steps you've done.

When you both hate everyone
but you can't help it because
you're Pisces.

When you lose your mates at a festival...

... but find your true people.

When you learn the hard way
that glamping just means the tent
is a different shape.

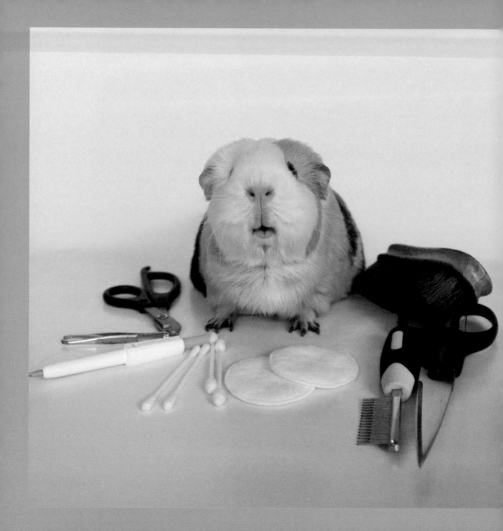

When HMRC asks what assets you have.

When you come
with baggage.

When fake tan is not your strong point.

When you go food shopping
on an empty stomach.

When you spend two hours making a wedding decoration then the bride says she wants 19 more.

When you've spent the evening laughing about your exes but now it's midnight and you need someone to text.

When it's 2006 and someone pokes you on Facebook.

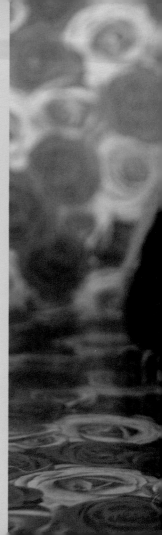

When you want to be a feminist but also a pretty, pretty princess.

When you're at a Michelin star restaurant and your main arrives.

When the whole restaurant sings 'Happy Birthday' and you have to pretend it isn't your worst nightmare.